Want more tips, tools, and resources to build your leadership development and coaching business? Check out **www.coachmetrix.com/resources** and **http://sccoaching.com/coachtraining/**

Stakeholder Centered Coaching®

Maximizing Your Impact as a Coach

Marshall Goldsmith and Sal Silvester

**Foreword by
Frank Wagner**

An Actionable Business Journal

E-mail: info@thinkaha.com
20660 Stevens Creek Blvd., Suite 210
Cupertino, CA 95014

⇨ Please go to http://aha.pub/SCCoaching to read this AHAbook and to share the individual AHAmessages that resonate with you.

Published by THiNKaha®
20660 Stevens Creek Blvd., Suite 210, Cupertino, CA 95014
http://thinkaha.com
E-mail: info@thinkaha.com

First Printing: February 2018
Hardcover ISBN: 978-1-61699-237-8 (1-61699-237-9)
Paperback ISBN: 978-1-61699-236-1 (1-61699-236-0)
eBook ISBN: 978-1-61699-235-4 (1-61699-235-2)
Place of Publication: Silicon Valley, California, USA
Paperback Library of Congress Number: 2017959870

Dedication

To our global coaching colleagues who are making this world a better place, one leader at a time.

Dedication

How to Read a THiNKaha® Book
A Note from the Publisher

The THiNKaha series is the CliffsNotes of the 21st century. The value of these books is that they are contextual in nature. Although the actual words won't change, their meaning will change every time you read one as your context will change. Experience your own "AHA!" moments ("AHAmessages™") with a THiNKaha book; AHAmessages are looked at as "actionable" moments—think of a specific project you're working on, an event, a sales deal, a personal issue, etc. and see how the AHAmessages in this book can inspire your own AHAmessages, something that you can specifically act on. Here's how to read one of these books and have it work for you:

1. Read a THiNKaha book (these slim and handy books should only take about 15-20 minutes of your time!) and write down one to three actionable items you thought of while reading it. Each journal-style THiNKaha book is equipped with space for you to write down your notes and thoughts underneath each AHAmessage.

2. Mark your calendar to re-read this book again in 30 days.

3. Repeat step #1 and write down one to three more AHAmessages that grab you this time. I guarantee that they will be different than the first time. BTW: this is also a great time to reflect on the actions taken from the last set of AHAmessages you wrote down.

After reading a THiNKaha book, writing down your AHAmessages, re-reading it, and writing down more AHAmessages, you'll begin to see how these books contextually apply to you. THiNKaha books advocate for continuous, lifelong learning. They will help you transform your ahas into actionable items with tangible results until you no longer have to say "AHA!" to these moments—they'll become part of your daily practice as you continue to grow and learn.

As The AHA Guy at THiNKaha, I definitely practice what I preach. I read 2-3 AHAbooks a month in addition to those that we publish and take away two to three different action items from each of them every time. Please e-mail me your AHAs today!

Mitchell Levy
publisher@thinkaha.com

Contents

Foreword

As long-time partners with Marshall Goldsmith, Chris Coffey and I have trained thousands of coaches on Marshall's behavioral coaching methodology. Since 2001, we've built the largest coaching network in the world and are helping leaders globally make positive and sustainable change. And as a practicing coach myself, I know the power of Stakeholder Centered Coaching® first hand.

In this AHAbook, you'll have a practical guide, organized in a way that will enhance your ability to coach using Marshall Goldsmith's proven methods, and more importantly, it will help your clients also learn what they can do to up their game as leaders.

For your clients, Stakeholder Centered Coaching® will help them make positive and measurable change that's recognized by others. Your clients, like any other leader trying to get better, can change in an instant, but there's always a gap between when they make a change and when others around them see that change. This AHAbook is designed as a tool to make it easier for leaders to turn what they know into what they do. With Stakeholder Centered Coaching®, your clients will learn how to engage others who are impacted by their behavior, follow up, and implement suggestions that will result in both behavior and perception change.

For you as a coach, this AHAbook will help reinforce the Stakeholder Centered Coaching® process and aid you in differentiating your coaching business by measuring change and demonstrating a return on investment to your executive sponsors. After all, executives pay for results, not coaching.

As a book designed for today's reality of precious little time to do even what is essential and important, *Stakeholder Centered*

Coaching is a refreshing and powerful way to reinforce the process of involving stakeholders in the task of helping effective leaders be better every year.

Frank Wagner
Partner in charge of Stakeholder Centered Coaching®
Marshall Goldsmith Group

Share the AHA messages from this book socially by going to
http://aha.pub/SCCoaching.

Section I

Stakeholder Centered Coaching Overview

Stakeholder Centered Coaching is a proven coaching methodology and philosophy created by Marshall Goldsmith that demonstrates ROI and dramatically increases the likelihood of a successful coaching engagement. Even better, it's a process you can use both personally and professionally for creating any kind of transformational change. Here's an overview on how the Stakeholder Centered Coaching process works.

1

#SCC (StakeholderCenteredCoaching) is a methodology created by Marshall Goldsmith, designed to make leaders effective. @Coachmetrix

_____

_____

_____

2

A major gap in #Leadership & executive coaching is the lack of measurement on whether a leader has evolved. #SCC @CoachGoldsmith

_____

_____

_____

3

US companies spend $14+ billion annually on #Leadership dev & most don't know if their efforts are successful. Do you? @Coachmetrix

_____

_____

_____

4

We can & must measure our coaching impact & #StakeholderCenteredCoaching is the way to do that. @Coachmetrix

_____

_____

_____

5

The #StakeholderCenteredCoaching process is designed to help people make positive and sustained behavior change. @CoachGoldsmith

_____

_____

_____

6

#Success isn't determined by the #Leader being coached, but by people impacted by their behavior. #SCC @CoachGoldsmith

_____

_____

_____

7

1 of 3 differentiators btwn #StakeholderCenteredCoaching & other coaching methodologies is the #Stakeholder emphasis. @CoachGoldsmith

_____

_____

_____

8

The #StakeholderCenteredCoaching process not only impacts the #Leader, it impacts the #Stakeholders supporting the Leader. @Coachmetrix

_____

_____

_____

9

In #StakeholderCenteredCoaching,
#Stakeholders are recruited as valued
members of the change process.
@CoachGoldsmith

_____

_____

_____

10

#Stakeholders are people who're impacted
by the Leader's behavior & willing to
support them on their #Change journey.
#SCC @Coachmetrix

_____

_____

_____

11

#Stakeholders' traits: being open minded, letting go of old perceptions & willing to change opinion about their leaders. @CoachGoldsmith

_____

_____

_____

12

Looking for #Stakeholders to support your #Change efforts? They could be anyone impacted by the #Leader's behaviors. #SCC @Coachmetrix

_____

_____

_____

13

2 of 3 differentiators in #StakeholderCenteredCoaching is the emphasis on feedforward. @CoachGoldsmith

_____

_____

_____

14

#Feedforward is providing ideas
& suggestions for the future.
#StakeholderCenteredCoaching
@Coachmetrix

_____

_____

_____

15

In #StakeholderCenteredCoaching,
#Feedforward shifts the focus from the past
to the future. How have you done this?
@Coachmetrix

16

In #SCC, stakeholders are asked to provide #Feedback & #Feedforward about their leader's performance. @Coachmetrix

_____

_____

_____

17

3 of 3 differentiators in #StakeholderCenteredCoaching is its focus on both #BehaviorChange & #PerceptionChange. @CoachGoldsmith

_____

_____

_____

18

In the leadership dev process, there's always a lag btwn when a #Leader changes & when others feel/see the change. #SCC @Coachmetrix

---

19

#StakeholderCenteredCoaching is a practical, relevant process that involves 5 key steps to deploy. Do you know them? @CoachGoldsmith

20

#StakeholderCenteredCoaching Step 1 of 5: #Leader identifies a clear development goal & Stakeholders. @Coachmetrix

21

#Leaders who choose their goal have a higher level of commitment to them. #StakeholderCenteredCoaching @Coachmetrix

_____

_____

_____

22

Online action plans are more transparent btwn the #Coach, #Leader & others who see it. Is your action plan process online? #SCC @Coachmetrix

_____

_____

_____

23

Leader's #Stakeholders should be calibrated with the Leader's manager to ensure the right Stakeholders are selected. #SCC @Coachmetrix

_____

_____

_____

24

Leader's goal calibration prevents a manager from saying at the end of the engagement that the Leader worked on the wrong goal.

_____

_____

_____

25

#Leaders should verbally enroll their #Stakeholders to ensure they understand their role. #StakeholderCenteredCoaching @CoachGoldsmith

_____

_____

_____

26

#StakeholderCenteredCoaching Step 2 of 5: #Leader goes public w/ their goals so #Stakeholders know what to observe. @CoachGoldsmith

_____

_____

_____

27

When a leader goes public with a plan, it serves as the example for others to do the same. #StakeholderCenteredCoaching @Coachmetrix

_____

_____

_____

28

#StakeholderCenteredCoaching Step 3 of 5:
Leader builds an action plan based on input
from #Stakeholders. @Coachmetrix

_____

_____

_____

29

In #SCC, the #Leaders plan is distributed to
#Stakeholders so they know what to look for
when providing input. @Coachmetrix

_____

_____

_____

30

#StakeholderCenteredCoaching Step 4 of 5:
#Leader follows up on a monthly basis with
#Stakeholders. @CoachGoldsmith

31

#Stakeholder follow-up provides #Leaders
with ideas to support change & helps close
the perception gap. #SCC @Coachmetrix

32

The #Leader & coach modify action plan for the coming month based on #Feedforward provided by the #Stakeholders. #SCC @CoachGoldsmith

_____

_____

_____

33

#StakeholderCenteredCoaching Step 5 of 5: #Leader formally measures results with #MiniSurveys of #Stakeholders. @Coachmetrix

---

34

The #MiniSurvey in #StakeholderCenteredCoaching measures progress on a scale of -3 through +3; 0 represents no change. @CoachGoldsmith

---

35

Coachmetrix is a cloud-based tool that optimizes the entire #SCC Process, including measurement. @CoachGoldsmith

_____

_____

_____

36

For a #Leader to be a successful coachee, they must be open to input and willing to change. #StakeholderCenteredCoaching @Coachmetrix

_____

_____

_____

37

#Leaders must possess three virtues in #StakeholderCenteredCoaching: courage, humility, and discipline. @CoachGoldsmith

38

1 of 6 #BehavioralCoachingSkills needed by a #Coach is ability to help the #Leader determine their coaching goals. #SCC @CoachGoldsmith

_____

_____

_____

39

For a coach to be a successful in #StakeholderCenteredCoaching, they need to be versed in #BehavioralCoachingSkills. @CoachGoldsmith #SCC

_____

_____

_____

40

In #StakeholderCenteredCoaching, goals
have a goal statement, a behavior to
measure/track change & action items.
@CoachGoldsmith

_____

_____

_____

41

In #SCC, managers calibrate the goals to ensure #Leaders are working on the right developmental areas. @CoachGoldsmith

_____

_____

_____

42

2 of 6 #BehavioralCoachingSkills needed is the ability to help the #Leader rehearse interactions w/ #Stakeholders. #SCC @CoachGoldsmith

_____

_____

_____

43

In #StakeholderCenteredCoaching, the coach can use video to enhance the rehearsing process btwn a leader & Stakeholders. @Coachmetrix

_____

_____

_____

44

3 of 6 #BehavioralCoachingSkills needed by a coach is the ability to help the #Leader create an action plan. #SCC @CoachGoldsmith

---

45

In #StakeholderCenteredCoaching, the coach helps translate #Stakeholders' suggestions into concrete action plans. @Coachmetrix

---

46

4 of 6 #BehavioralCoachingSkills needed by a coach is the ability to reinforce #Positive change. #SCC @CoachGoldsmith

_____

_____

_____

47

5 of 6 #BehavioralCoachingSkills is to conduct after-action assessments to help #Leaders learn from their experience. #SCC @Coachmetrix

_____

_____

_____

48

The #AfterActionAssessment is a process developed by the military to assess learnings and includes 4 questions. #SCC @CoachGoldsmith

_____

_____

_____

49

The #AfterActionAssessment Question 1
of 4: What did you intend to do in the last
30 days? #StakeholderCenteredCoaching
@Coachmetrix

50

The #AfterActionAssessment Question
2 of 4: What actually happened?
#StakeholderCenteredCoaching
@Coachmetrix

_____

_____

_____

51

The #AfterActionAssessment Question
3 of 4: What did you learn? Or are you
learning? #StakeholderCenteredCoaching
@CoachGoldsmith

_____

_____

_____

52

The #AfterActionAssessment Question
4 of 4: What are your next steps?
#StakeholderCenteredCoaching
@CoachGoldsmith

_____

_____

_____

53

6 of 6 #BehavioralCoachingSkills is the
ability to tell stories to create teachable
moments for the #Leader. #SCC
@CoachGoldsmith

_____

_____

_____

54

In #SCC, a coach needs to help the #Leader navigate how to deal with conflicting feedback from their #Stakeholders. @Coachmetrix

_____

_____

_____

55

Improved #Leadership drives
better business results &
communication within the company.
#StakeholderCenteredCoaching
@Coachmetrix

Share the AHA messages from this book socially by going to
http://aha.pub/SCCoaching.

Section II

#StartSmart

Getting the right foundation in place is critical for any leadership and executive coaching process. Here are the key steps to start smart on your Stakeholder Centered Coaching engagement so there is clear alignment and trust between the coach and leader, clarity on what the leader will focus on throughout the engagement, and understanding of how Stakeholders will be engaged throughout the process.

56

A #StakeholderCenteredCoaching process should #StartSmart. How do you do this on your coaching engagements? @CoachGoldsmith

_____

_____

_____

57

1 of 4 #StartSmart Steps: Every #StakeholderCenteredCoaching engagement starts with clear coaching agreements. @CoachGoldsmith

_____

_____

_____

58

#StartSmartCoaching agreements ensure that the #Leader knows what to expect from their coach & themselves as the coachee. @Coachmetrix

_____

_____

_____

59

2 of 4 #StartSmart Steps: Select a behavior to develop. #StakeholderCenteredCoaching @Coachmetrix

_____

_____

_____

60

When #DataGathering for #Leader's effectiveness, use a verbal or online 360 method. #StakeholderCenteredCoaching @Coachmetrix

_____

_____

_____

61

#360Raters should be selected by the
#Leader so they accept their input as valid.
#StakeholderCenteredCoaching
@Coachmetrix

_____

_____

_____

62

#Leaders verbally enroll #Stakeholders
to ensure they understand their role.
#StakeholderCenteredCoaching
@CoachGoldsmith

_____

_____

_____

63

#Stakeholders need to provide ongoing
#Feedback & #Feedforward with a specific
focus on the future. #SCC @Coachmetrix

_____

_____

_____

64

#Stakeholders need to have an open mind, let go of old notions of #Leader & be able to change their opinions. #SCC @CoachGoldsmith

_____

_____

_____

65

The #Coach helps the #Leader prioritize their developmental goal(s). #StakeholderCenteredCoaching @CoachGoldsmith

_____

_____

_____

66

A #DevelopmentGoal can be easily updated & shared between the #Leader, Coach & #Stakeholders when it's online. #SCC @Coachmetrix

---

67

In #SCC, #Coaches must help #Leaders navigate contradictory data that may arise during the data collection process. @Coachmetrix

---

68

3 of 4 #StartSmart steps:
#StakeholderCenteredCoaching is to
help the #Leader select the appropriate
#Stakeholders. @CoachGoldsmith

_____

_____

_____

69

#SCC #Leaders can choose different
#Stakeholders for each goal if they have
multiple developmental goals.
@Coachmetrix

_____

_____

_____

70

4 of 4 #StartSmart steps: Ensure that the #Leader's goals & #Stakeholders are calibrated with the Leader's manager. #SCC @Coachmetrix

_____

_____

_____

71

In #StartSmart, calibrating with the #Leader's manager helps ensure alignment with organizational goals. #SCC
@Coachmetrix

_____

_____

_____

72

The #StakeholderCenteredCoaching process not only impacts the #Leader but also #Stakeholders supporting the Leader.
@Coachmetrix

_____

_____

_____

Share the AHA messages from this book socially by going to
http://aha.pub/SCCoaching.

Section III

Implementing Stakeholder Suggestions

Stakeholders play a critical role in helping a leader change. This section addresses how the leader will work with Stakeholders to gather their input, implement their suggestions, and ultimately, change both behavior and perceptions. Both are critical to a leader's success.

73

After the #StartSmart #StakeholderCenteredCoaching process, #Leaders need to start #Implementing #Stakeholder suggestions. @Coachmetrix

_____

_____

_____

74

The coach in #StakeholderCenteredCoaching helps #Leaders see the benefit of changing & the cost if they don't. @CoachGoldsmith

_____

_____

_____

75

The cost of not changing #Stakeholders' perceptions may affect the #Leader's career, those around them & the business. #SCC @Coachmetrix

---

76

#Leaders should speak with #Stakeholders on a monthly basis to gather their #Feedback & #Feedforward. #SCC @CoachGoldsmith

---

77

#Leaders need to model feedback response, responding with appreciation & commitment to improvement. #SCC @CoachGoldsmith

_____

_____

_____

78

#FeedbackReactions: People have different emotional reactions to change upon receiving feedback. How do you react? #SCC @Coachmetrix

_____

_____

_____

79

#ReceivingFeedback takes both courage
& humility on the part of a #Leader.
#StakeholderCenteredCoaching
@Coachmetrix

_____

_____

_____

80

#Leaders' action plans should be based
on suggestions from #Stakeholders. Stay
focused & don't take on too much. #SCC
@Coachmetrix

_____

_____

_____

81

#Stakeholders will stay enrolled when they see a #Leader making a commitment to #Change. How do you drive commitment? #SCC @Coachmetrix

_____

_____

_____

82

Asking for #StakeholderFeedback: Leader needs to be brief, positive & focused. #StakeholderCenteredCoaching @Coachmetrix

_____

_____

_____

83

#Vulnerability is part of #Feedback & #Change; as a #Leader models this, it gives others permission too. #SCC @Coachmetrix

TRANSPARENCY GROWS TRUST IMPACTING ALL.

84

NEW PATTERNS

#Leaders are successful when others see leaders changing & not returning to old habits. #StakeholderCenteredCoaching @Coachmetrix

_____

_____

_____

85

#Leaders have to be willing to put on
new leadership hats, even if it doesn't feel
authentic or comfortable at first. #SCC
@Coachmetrix

_____

_____

_____

86

#SupportLeaders: consistently work on making the new behavior a habit w/ daily reminders, support, structure, etc. #SCC @Coachmetrix

_____

_____

_____

87

How should you respond to #Feedback and #Feedforward? Best way would be: Thank you! #StakeholderCenteredCoaching @CoachGoldsmith

_____

_____

_____

88

In #SSC, #AfterActionAssessment is
designed to reinforce progress and
learnings during coaching sessions.
@CoachGoldsmith

_____

_____

_____

89

In #SCC, #Coaching the #ActionPlan remains dynamic, changing month to month based on what's learned from #Stakeholders. @CoachGoldsmith

_____

_____

_____

90

#Stakeholders all receive revised action plans so they know what to observe in the #Leaders they're supporting. #SCC @CoachGoldsmith

_____

_____

_____

91

#Listening: What did #Stakeholders say/ not say to help #Leader gain insights & apply new actions? #SCC @Coachmetrix

[handwritten: ?! KEY FORWARD]

_____

_____

_____

92

#Stakeholder Follow-up: #Coach to help #Leader stay on track with monthly follow-ups with #Stakeholders. #SCC @Coachmetrix

_____

_____

_____

93

#Stakeholder Checkin: #Leaders are to find regular & consistent times to check in with #Stakeholders each month. #SCC @Coachmetrix

_____

_____

_____

94

Spend quality time coaching your #Leader
to review their last month's actions & plans
for the next 30 days. #SCC
@CoachGoldsmith

_____

_____

_____

95

In the words of @KenBlanchard, catch
the #Leader doing something right!
#StakeholderCenteredCoaching
@Coachmetrix

_____

_____

_____

96

#Stakeholder #FollowUpProcess: For monthly check-ins use a mix of mediums: in-person, video chat, phone, email, etc. #SCC @Coachmetrix

97

#Motivation Coach: Keep your #Leader motivated by highlighting where they've been successful. #SCC @CoachGoldsmith

_____

_____

_____

Share the AHA messages from this book socially by going to
http://aha.pub/SCCoaching.

Section IV

Sustaining Success

A leader can make a change in an instant, but making the change a reality over time is more difficult. In this next section, we'll explore how measurement, after-action assessments, recognition, and technology such as Coachmetrix will help sustain success.

98

After implementing #Stakeholder suggestions, you need to #SustainSuccess. How do you help your #Leaders sustain success? @CoachGoldsmith

_____

_____

_____

99

#StakeholderCenteredCoaching measures #BehaviorChange unlike other coaching systems. How do you measure behavior change? @Coachmetrix

_____

_____

_____

100

#StakeholderCenteredCoaching uses a #MiniSurvey as a formal way of measuring #BehaviorChange. Do you use this tool? @Coachmatrix

_____

_____

_____

101

The #MiniSurvey is conducted a few times during a year-long coaching engagement. #StakeholderCenteredCoaching @Coachmetrix

_____

_____

_____

102

Continually measure the #Leader's progress against their goals from the #Stakeholders' perspective. #MiniSurvey #SCC @Coachmetrix

_____

_____

_____

103

A #MiniSurvey is typically a 7-point scale from -3 through +3, where 0 represents no change. #SCC @CoachGoldsmith

_____

_____

_____

104

#AfterActionAssessment: Coach meets w/ the #Leader to discuss the #MiniSurvey results. #SCC @CoachGoldsmith

_____

_____

_____

105

#Leaders should formally write out an #AfterActionAssessment to foster learning. #StakeholderCenteredCoaching @Coachmetrix

_____

_____

_____

106

Follow-up: #Leaders thank Stakeholders for their time & #Feedback after reviewing the #MiniSurvey results. #SCC @CoachGoldsmith

_____

_____

_____

107

Remind the #Leader: The most useful tool in changing behavior & perception is the monthly checkins w/ #Stakeholders. #SCC @Coachmetrix

_____

_____

_____

108

#Leader development: On many engagements, the written #AfterActionAssessment is shared with the Leader's manager. #SCC @CoachGoldsmith

---

109

Reinforce behavioral skills by spotting improvement in the #leader & providing appropriate recognition. #SCC @CoachGoldsmith

---

110

#SCC: There are many ways to add to the standard process using your unique coaching skills. What have you done? @Coachmetrix

_____

_____

_____

111

Additions to the #StakeholderCenteredCoaching process: Observe the #leader in the workplace. @Coachmetrix

_____

_____

_____

112

Additions to the standard #StakeholderCenteredCoaching process: Tell stories to enhance learning. @CoachGoldsmith

_____

_____

_____

113

Additions to the
#StakeholderCenteredCoaching process:
Follow up with #Stakeholders using
confidential interviews. @Coachmetrix

_____

_____

_____

114

Additions to #SCC: Conduct a second
calibration coaching session with the
#Leader & manager to align next steps.
@Coachmetrix

_____

_____

_____

115

Additions to #SCC: Help the #Leader uncover limiting mindsets, assumptions & beliefs that drive derailing behavior. @Coachmetrix

_____

_____

_____

116

Additions to #SCC: Leverage your own coaching skills and tools to supplement the process. @Coachmetrix

_____

_____

_____

117

Support high-performing #Leaders in recognizing their strengths; they often focus only on their deficits. #SCC @Coachmetrix

---

118

#Coaches who regularly ask for #Feedback & #Feedforward from #Leaders are modeling the #SCC process. @Coachmetrix

_____

_____

_____

119

#SCC final #MiniSurvey happens toward the end of the coaching engagement; it's an important conclusion to the process.
@CoachGoldsmith

_____

_____

_____

120

Beyond Coaching Engagement: Debrief the final #MiniSurvey results with the #Leader and focus on #NextSteps. #SCC
@Coachmetrix

_____

_____

_____

121

#SCC final #MiniSurvey validates the progress the #Leader has made over the course of the #Coaching engagement. @Coachmetrix

_____

_____

_____

122

#Coaches ensure their #Leaders have thanked their #Stakeholders for support throughout their coaching engagement. #SCC @Coachmetrix

_____

_____

_____

123

#Coaches have their #Leaders document an #AfterActionAssessment based on the results of their #Coaching engagement. #SCC @Coachmetrix

_____

_____

_____

124

#Coaches reinforce to #Leaders that they are now able to do the process on their own with any #BehavioralChange. #SCC @CoachGoldsmith

_____

_____

_____

125

To #SustainSuccess,
#StakeholderCenteredCoaching coaches
celebrate successes. How do you celebrate?
@Coachmetrix

_____

_____

_____

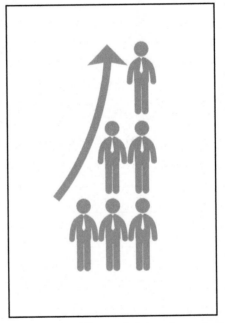

Share the AHA messages from this book socially by going to
http://aha.pub/SCCoaching.

Section V

Using Stakeholder Centered Coaching with Teams

Stakeholder Centered Coaching is as effective with teams as it is with individual leaders. Learn more about how you can build teams without wasting time.

126

#StakeholderCenteredCoaching is an outstanding process for helping #Teams reach new levels of success. @Coachmetrix

_____

_____

_____

127

#SCC can be used with newly formed teams, cross-functional teams, teams working through dysfunctions, and others. @CoachGoldsmith

_____

_____

_____

128

In #SCC, the focus shifts from the individual to the #Team & the core principles remain the same. @Coachmetrix

_____

_____

_____

129

The #Coach helps the #Team
select a goal for development.
#StakeholderCenteredCoaching
@CoachGoldsmith

_____

_____

_____

130

The #Team creates an action
plan to move their goal forward.
#StakeholderCenteredCoaching
@Coachmetrix

_____

_____

_____

131

Individual #Team members select a
goal in support of the overall team goal.
#StakeholderCenteredCoaching
@CoachGoldsmith

_____

_____

_____

132

The #Coach conducts quick monthly check-in coaching calls with #Team Members. #StakeholderCenteredCoaching @Coachmetrix

_____

_____

_____

133

Coaching all team members gives the #Coach a unique perspective that will enable them to make a bigger difference. #SCC @Coachmetrix

_____

_____

_____

134

The #Coach can do an optional step & meet
w/ the team on a monthly basis to review
progress against its dev goal. #SCC
@CoachGoldsmith

_____

_____

_____

135

Monthly meetings w/ the #Coach also enables the #Team to adjust its next 30-day action plan. #StakeholderCenteredCoaching @Coachmetrix

_____

_____

_____

136

#Team members can do their monthly check-ins during a regularly scheduled team meeting. #StakeholderCenteredCoaching @Coachmetrix

_____

_____

_____

137

#Coaches conduct #MiniSurveys during the coaching engagement to evaluate progress. #StakeholderCenteredCoaching @CoachGoldsmith

_____

_____

_____

138

#Coaches meet w/ the #Team Leader
& Sponsor throughout the coaching
engagement to reinforce process & share
results. #SCC @Coachmetrix

139

For additional #SCC development ideas,
refer to @CoachGoldsmith's book, "What
Got You Here Won't Get You There."
@Coachmetrix

140

The #StakeholderCenteredCoaching
process effectively turns your #Stakeholders
into your #Coaches. @CoachGoldsmith

About the Authors

Dr. Marshall Goldsmith is the author or editor of thirty-five books that have sold over two million copies, been translated into thirty languages, and become bestsellers in twelve countries. Marshall's professional acknowledgments include: "World's #1 Leadership Thinker" from *Harvard Business Review* and *Best Practices Institute*; "World's #1 Executive Coach" from *Global Gurus, INC* and *Fast Company* magazines; "Lifetime Achievement Award for Excellence in Teaching" from Institute for Management Studies; "50 great thinkers and leaders who have influenced the field of management over the past 80 years" from American Management Association; "50 great leaders in America" from *BusinessWeek*; "Top ten executive educators" from *Wall Street Journal*; "Most credible executive advisors in the new era of business" from *Economist* (UK); "Fellow of the Academy (America's top HR award)" from National Academy of Human Resources; and "Global leader in HR thinking" from World HRD Congress (India). His work has been recognized by almost every professional organization in his field.

Sal Silvester is one of the top experts on leadership transformations across organizations and throughout careers. He is the founder and president of 5.12 Solutions Consulting Group, a firm that supports leaders and teams through grounded, real-world practices and techniques. Their cloud-based coaching platform, Coachmetrix, is the first of its kind to optimize and measure leadership development programs and coaching engagements. His passion and expertise for working with teams and leaders is reflected in his coaching, writing, and speaking keynotes. As the author of *Ignite! The 4 Essential Rules for Emerging Leaders* and *Unite! The 4 Mindset Shifts for Senior Leaders*, Silvester uses learning parables and his proprietary People-First Leadership™ Model to explain the secrets to making the transition from peer to leader. His unique perspective has been nurtured through his experience over the past 25 years as an Army Officer, an executive at Accenture, and as the founder of 5.12 Solutions and Coachmetrix.

AHAthat makes it easy to share, author, and promote content. There are over 40,000 quotes (AHAmessages™) by thought leaders from around the world that you can share in seconds for free.

For those who want to author their own book, we have time-tested proven processes that allow you to write your AHAbook™ of 140 digestible, bite-sized morsels in eight hours or less. Once your content is on AHAthat, you have a customized link that you can use to have your fans/advocates share your content and help grow your network.

⮑ Start sharing: **http://AHAthat.com**

⮑ Start authoring: **http://AHAthat.com/Author**

Please go directly to this book in AHAthat and share each AHAmessage socially at
http://aha.pub/SCCoaching.

CPSIA information can be obtained
at www.ICGtesting.com
Printed in the USA
BVOW11s0400200318
511050BV00004B/17/P